B A$+

ACT 6349

Gentle, Victor.

J
599.6655   Florida
GEN   Cracker horses

SANTA CRUZ CITY-COUNTY LIBRARY SYSTEM

0000115190209

DISCARD

8/2008

D1123412

SANTA CRUZ PUBLIC LIBRARY
Santa Cruz, California

GREAT AMERICAN

HORSES

AN IMAGINATION LIBRARY SERIES

FLORIDA CRACKER
HORSES

by Victor Gentle and Janet Perry

Gareth Stevens Publishing
A WORLD ALMANAC EDUCATION GROUP COMPANY

Special thanks to Dewaine and Doyle Hazellief for taking time to patiently teach us a thing or a thousand about crackers.

—Victor Gentle and Janet Perry

Please visit our web site at: www.garethstevens.com
For a free color catalog describing Gareth Stevens' list of high-quality books and
multimedia programs, call 1-800-542-2595 (USA) or 1-800-461-9120 (Canada).
Gareth Stevens Publishing's Fax: (414) 332-3567.

Library of Congress Cataloging-in-Publication Data

Gentle, Victor.
    Florida Cracker horses / by Victor Gentle and Janet Perry.
        p. cm. — (Great American horses: an imagination library series)
    Includes bibliographical references (p. 23) and index.
    ISBN 0-8368-2936-0 (lib. bdg.)
    1. Florida cracker horse—Juvenile literature. [1. Florida cracker horse. 2. Horses.]
    I. Perry, Janet, 1960- II. Title.
    SF293.F55G46   2001
    599.665'5—dc21   2001020852

First published in 2001 by
Gareth Stevens Publishing
A World Almanac Education Group Company
330 West Olive Street, Suite 100
Milwaukee, WI 53212 USA

Text: Victor Gentle and Janet Perry
Page layout: Victor Gentle, Janet Perry, and Scott M. Krall
Cover design: Renee M. Bach
Series editor: Katherine J. Meitner
Picture researcher: Diane Laska-Swanke

Photo credits: Cover, pp. 5, 7, 9, 11, 13, 15, 17, 19, 21, 22 © Bob Langrish

This edition © 2001 by Gareth Stevens, Inc. All rights reserved to Gareth Stevens, Inc. No part of
this book may be reproduced, stored in a retrieval system, or transmitted in any form or by any means,
electronic, mechanical, photocopying, recording, or otherwise, without the prior written permission
of the publisher except for the inclusion of brief quotations in an acknowledged review.

Printed in the United States of America

1 2 3 4 5 6 7 8 9 05 04 03 02 01

Front cover: A Florida Cracker Horse herd. Most horses in the wild form this kind of group, called a harem, usually with two to twelve **mares** for every **stallion**.

TABLE OF CONTENTS

Words that appear in the glossary are printed in **boldface** type the first time they occur in the text.

CATCH A BLUE HORSE

Blue, a two-year-old **colt**, outsmarted Dewaine Hazellief and his dad, Doyle, in a thick north Florida forest for five hours. His bluish-gray coat hid him in the shadows of oak and palmetto trees.

The poor horse was terrified. Because he was a young male, the stallions beat him up. Alone, he was prey for panthers. Each time Blue saw Dewaine and his dad, he froze. Each time they got close enough for him to hear their horses' chuffing breath, Blue let out a squeal. Then he left them with the sound of his hooves thudding away. After many escapes, they finally caught him.

Doyle named him "Ayer's Blue." "Ayers" came from John Law Ayers, who owned the land he was roped on. "Blue" came from the color of his coat.

Dewaine Hazellief practices riding Ayers Blue without a bridle. Dewaine just leans a little bit in the saddle, and that's the way Blue goes.

FIRST CRACKS

Ayers Blue — the name tells a story. There are many names given to Blue's **breed**, each one telling a little about the history of Florida Cracker Horses and the people who **bred** them.

Between 1521 and the mid-1600s, Spanish explorers, invaders, and settlers brought the first modern horses to America. They brought these horses to help them drive cattle and explore the New World. Since the feed was poor and the work was long and hard, the best horses had to be small and tough.

While Florida is no longer new to Cracker Horses, generations of foals have looked upon the prairies, marshes, and woods of Florida with new eyes.

GIFT HORSES

The early Spanish ranchers of Florida quickly became known for the sharp cracking of their whips as they gathered their cows and drove their herds. The cracking sound is the reason why the ranchers, their cattle, and their horses were called "**crackers**."

Native Americans did not welcome Spanish ranchers invading their land. Sometimes after a fight, the ranchers were forced to flee the land in a hurry, leaving their horses behind.

The Native Americans did, however, welcome the fine animals! They carefully bred their own herds. That is why the Florida Cracker Horse was also known as the "Seminole" or "Chickasaw" pony.

A modern **cowhunter** and his Cracker Horse cut a cow from the herd, as their ancestors have done for the last 400 years.

A HORSE BY MANY NAMES

Some Cracker Horses escaped from people. They formed wild herds over time and became a part of Florida's wildlife. In fact, many Cracker Horses were named after the places where they lived.

The horses that lived in the northern marshes between Jacksonville and the state line of Georgia were called "marsh tackies." In the prairies south of Gainesville, they were known as "prairie ponies." Cracker Horses easily hid in the thick pine forests near Fort Myers. The local people called them "woods ponies."

In the 1900s, Florida became a vacation spot. Visitors thought the wild herds were native, so they called them "Florida horses" or "Florida cow ponies."

This horse may look chubby, but her belly is just extra full of salt grasses and water. Another name for a Cracker Horse is "grass guts."

A DIAMOND IN THE ROUGH

Whatever they are called and wherever they live, Cracker Horses have the same fine qualities. If you saw a Cracker Horse running wild, all shaggy, muddy, and terrified, you might not think it was such a treasure. Like their wild cousins in Spain, they have unusual strength and endurance. They also learn quickly and have fancy gaits bred into them.

A gait is the way that a horse moves. Most horses walk, trot, canter, lope, and gallop. A trot is a kind of jog. The canter and lope are slow runs. The gallop is a fast-as-you-can-go run. Some horses have even more gaits!

This trotting Cracker Horse's short back, sturdy body, and strong, straight legs are good qualities for a riding horse to have.

TREASURE TROVE

Some Cracker Horses are born with the ability to do a **running walk**, which is a very fast walk that is easy to ride all day. A few horses are born with what some folks call the "coon rack," which is a very fast gait where, at times, only one of the horse's feet is on the ground.

The coon rack got its name because **cowhunters** liked riding this smooth gait to go hunting for raccoons, rabbits, and squirrels.

Like their Spanish relatives, Cracker Horses are light with elegant looks. They are 13.5 to 15 **hands** high and weigh from 750 to 1,000 pounds (340 to 454 kilograms). Cracker Horses are the perfect size for the fast turns and quick stops that cattle horses must do.

Cracker Horses wear many of the colors found on horses around the world. This pretty stallion is a gray dapple color.

TREASURING THE PAST

From the 1500s to the 1930s, there were so many herds of Cracker Horses that Floridians took them for granted. By the 1980s, hardly any land was left for the wild herds. Cracker Horses had almost disappeared. Young cowhunters were riding Quarter Horses instead of Cracker Horses, since a trained Cracker Horse wasn't worth any more money than a wild one.

Billy Davis, Sam Getzen, and John Ayers knew that the Cracker Horse breed was treasure, not trash. In 1985, they formed the Florida Cracker Horse Association to preserve the breed and its contribution to Florida's history.

Cowhunters often teach their horses tricks. Here, Billy Davis shifts his weight back, which tells his horse to back up and spin around.

CRACKERJACK COWHUNTERS

Like most other hardworking cowhunters, Dewaine works eight hours or more each day with Blue. Together, they hunt, **hem**, herd, rope, doctor, and **brand** cows. On weekends, they might go to a show, where they do these same things to win ribbons and prize money.

Cracker Horses are also good trail horses. When some other horses are tuckered out after competition, the Cracker Horses are just warming up.

Dewaine knew Cracker Horses were good horses, but he thought they would be a waste of his time. Now he is glad that his dad talked him into catching and training one.

A group of riders are happy to be trail riding on their Cracker Horses.

A BLUE GEM OF A HORSE

A Florida cowhunter's motto is, "If we catch it, we mean to keep it, and *whatever comes along with it*." Dewaine Hazellief lived by that motto as he taught Ayers Blue to be a gentle cow horse.

What came along with training Blue were somersaults, bucking, broken ribs, bruises, and a brush or two with death. Even so, Dewaine trained Blue carefully and kindly. First, he got Blue to trust him. Finally, Blue could do everything that Dewaine asked him to do, from standing steady with a rope tied to a steer to driving cows without a bridle.

After four years, Dewaine had polished the rough and ready Blue into a gem of a cow horse.

"We just wanted to show that a little Cracker Horse could do anything any other cow horse could do, and more," said Doyle Hazellief.

DIAGRAM AND SCALE OF A HORSE

Here's how to measure a horse with a show of hands.
This Florida Cracker Horse is built nicely for long days
on the range, with its short back and sturdy shoulders.

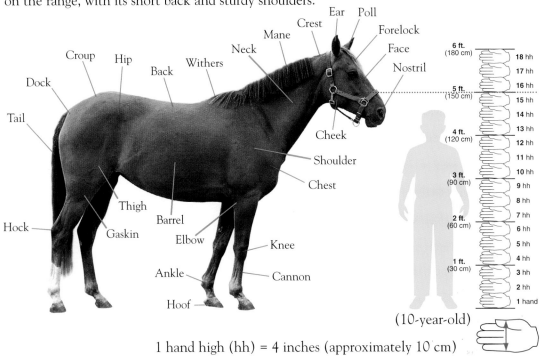

1 hand high (hh) = 4 inches (approximately 10 cm)

(10-year-old)

WHERE TO WRITE OR CALL FOR MORE INFORMATION

Florida Cracker Horse Association, Inc.
P.O. Box 186
Newberry, FL 32669
Phone: (352) 472-2228

MORE TO READ AND VIEW

Books (Fiction):   *Classic Horse and Pony Stories.* Edited by Diana Pullein-Thompson (Dorling Kindersley)

Books (Nonfiction):   *The Complete Guides to Horses and Ponies* (series). Jackie Budd (Gareth Stevens)
DK Riding Club: Horse and Pony Breeds. Carolyn Henderson (Dorling Kindersley)
Great American Horses (series). Victor Gentle and Janet Perry (Gareth Stevens)
The United States Pony Club Manual of Horsemanship: Basics for Beginners. Susan E. Harris (Hungry Minds)
Wild Horse Magic for Kids. Mark Henckel (Gareth Stevens)

Magazines: *Horse Illustrated* and its new magazine for young readers, *Young Rider*

Videos (Nonfiction):   *Eyewitness: Horse.* (BBC Lionheart/DK Vision)
The Noble Horse. (National Geographic)
Ultimate Guide to Horses. (Discovery Channel)

WEB SITES

Florida Cracker Horse Association:
www.imh.org/imh/bw/flcrack.html

For general horse information:
www.ansi.okstate.edu/breeds/horses

For more general horse information:
www.henry.k12.ga.us/pges/kid-pages/
horse-mania/index.htm
horsefun.com/facts/factfldr/facts.html

Some web sites stay current longer than others. To find additional web sites, use a reliable search engine, such as Yahooligans or KidsClick! (http://sunsite.berkeley.edu/KidsClick!/), with one or more of the following key words to help you locate information about horses: *Cracker Horses, dressage, Florida cow horses, gaits,* and *ranch.*

GLOSSARY

You can find these words on the pages listed. Reading a word in a sentence helps you understand it even better.

brand — to mark so as to show ownership 18

breed (n) — horses that share the same features as a result of careful selection of stallions and mares to mate 6, 16

breed (past tense **bred**) (v) — to choose stallions and mares with certain features to make foals with similar features 6, 8, 12

colt — a male horse under four years old 4

cowhunter — a person who finds, gathers, ropes, and marks cattle 8, 14, 16, 18, 20

cracker — a name for an early rancher in Florida. Their cattle and horses are also called crackers 8

hand — a unit used to measure horses. It is equal to 4 inches (10.2 cm), about the width of a human hand 14, 22

hem — to surround cattle with horses and dogs 18

mare — an adult female horse 2

running walk — a smooth fast walk, about two-and-a-half to five times faster than an ordinary walk 14

stallion — an adult male horse 2, 4, 14

INDEX

_0209